THE ARTIST WHO MADE YOU

Evie Moses

The Artist Who Made You

Copyright © 2022 by Evie Moses

This is a work of fiction. Names, characters, places, and incidents are either the product of the author's imagination or are used fictitiously, and any resemblance to actual persons, living or dead, business establishments, events, or locales is entirely coincidental.

Publisher
Yvonne Moses

Book Formatting and Editing
DHBonner Virtual Solutions, LLC
www.dhbonner.net

ISBN (English Version): 978-1-7348957-4-2
ISBN (Spanish Version): 978-1-7348957-5-9
ISBN Hardcover: 978-1-7348957-6-6

Published in the United States of America

Dedicated to all of God's little creations…
His perfect work is what you are.

The Artist painted the land
with the waters in the sky.

Wow! How amazing,
this I tell you is no lie.

He painted the flowers and the trees all the animals from birds to bees.

He took a rest and then approved all that He had made.

He thought something was missing so, through your mother's womb you came...

because he painted Daddy and Mommy to lovingly create.

It was how He designed it and not for us to change.

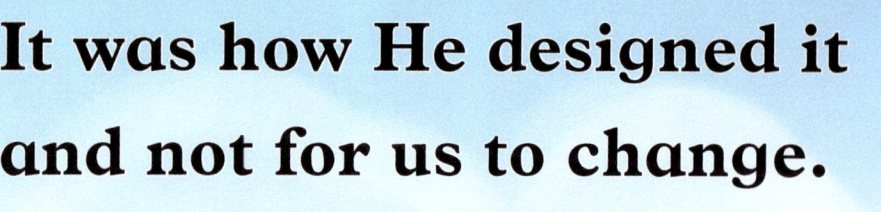

He's proud of His creation so wonderfully made...

Uniquely produced of different texture, tones, and shades.

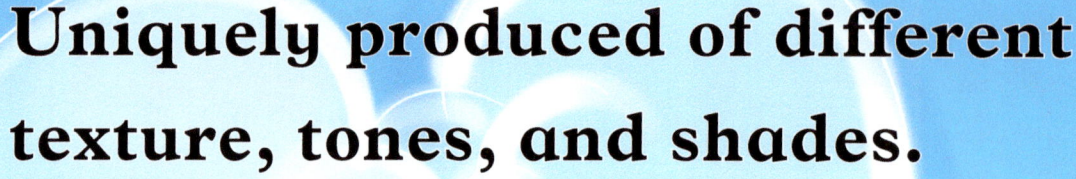

He made you so beautiful
to compliment Himself,
so that you wouldn't need to change
or look like someone else.

Who is this artist self-proclaimed?

This Artist is God...
God is His name.

He is large and in charge for all to seek.
He is the master and you are His masterpiece.

How lovely you are just as He made you.

A Note from the Author

I've experienced that my peace is contingent upon my reliance of God's standards. Because He is the artist, our creator, He knows what our needs are and can provide all that is necessary to fulfill them.

> Children are precious,
> They're born as a blessing.
> They look to us for guidance
> In a complex life directing.

God, All knowing,

We follow His lead…

To get better end results

For all our children's needs.

Look to Him for guidance

In rearing those little minds.

No one knows them better,

His creation so divine.

Other books by Evie Moses:

"Act Like a Parent, Think Like a Child"

"All Souls Matter: A Crash Course in Eternal Affairs"

www.ingramcontent.com/pod-product-compliance
Lightning Source LLC
Chambersburg PA
CBHW061402090426
42743CB00002B/118